1974

This book may be kept

FOURTEEN DAYS

A fine will be charged for each day the book is kept overtime.

GAYLORD 142			PRINTED IN U.S.A.

AFTER BORGES

AFTER BORGES

A Sequence of New Poems by R. H. W. Dillard

No true composer will take his substance from another
finite being—but there are times when he feels that
his self-expression needs some liberation from at least a part
of his own soul. At such times, shall he not better turn
to those greater souls, rather than to the external,
the immediate, and the 'Garish Day'?
    —Charles Ives

Louisiana State University Press

BATON ROUGE   1972

ISBN 0-8071-0233-4
Library of Congress Catalog Card Number 72-83036
Copyright © 1972 by R. H. W. Dillard
All rights reserved
Manufactured in the United States of America
Printed by Kingsport Press, Inc., Kingsport, Tennessee
Designed by Dwight Agner

Some of these poems appeared in the following publications, to
which grateful acknowledgement is made: *The American Scholar,
Contemporary Poetry in America, The Film Journal, The Hollins
Critic, Mill Mountain Review, Spectrum,* and *TriQuarterly.*

The author wishes to thank Frank McCullough for
his help with the translation of the Spanish poems
of Jorge Luis Borges.

To
Jorge Luis Borges
con cariño y estima

Contents

AFTER BORGES

Round Ruby

Round as pipes,
Round Ruby is corpulent
As kumquats, as a kumquat,
The kumquats in the red bowl
Where the sun opens the window,
Unravels last night like an equinox,
Reveals oranges, figs, the piano
In the hall, singed buckles
On the fireman's coat,
Corpuscular, brash, alive,
Bright as Round Ruby,
Round as a pipe,
Like today,
Tomorrow,
Round Ruby.

What Can You Say to Shoes

"What can you say to shoes,"
Tongues loose as leather,
Laces loose, sprawling
By the sofa, one lazing
Across the toe of the other?

An oblong of sunlight
Dusts the blue rug,
Indolent as shoes,
Taking its time.

The woolly sock offers
To muffle the silence,
A comforting solution.

You leave the room
(Annie) on naked feet
As shy as shadows
And close the door
With the finality
Of a rubber heel.

Sweet Strawberries

Like wet windows
On an open day. Skin knows.

The color punctuates
The shadows, the patches
Of hot sun.

No bitter core, the vine
Knows the ground
Like grass.

The taste lingers
Like touch.

Like leopards' eyes
Ignite the trees
Around the fire.

This I know:

Who loves me.

Wings

A celebration:

The wing of a bird, a shadow
That severs a bright day
Leaving it bright, a sparrow's
Wing, sooty, a sooty tern's,
Bright and white as the day
The sparrow split, a hawk's,
An eagle's, a wren's,
Wings that iron the air
And ring the ear, birds.

A package of cigarettes
With a card enclosed,
A shiny P-40 (more wings)

Against a blue and birdless
Sky, a wing of new smoke.

A trip to the moon.

The last two crisp wings
Beside the lonely neck
In the platter at the center
Of Sunday's spattered table,
The napkins crumpled
And greasy, scattered
On the linen like wings.

The wings of angels
Bending low.

The invisible wings of insects
Confusing the eye, evading
The swallow, the phoebe,
Scattered across the sill,
Along the sunny floor,
A dry variety of veins.

Dawn's wing, day's wing,
Wing of the eye that folds
The day to sleep, wing
Of the flying fish, the squirrel,
Wing of your house, your chair,
Of the stage, of the weather vane,
Wing of the maple's fruit,
Of the ash, the organ of flight,
An extension of the mind.

Winging it.

The Second Death

Breaking out of ground
Like fire, like weeds
Nodding in the early air,
Like water on a still day.

The dead are uneasy
And difficult, swaying

Over the rowboat's stern,
The long grey hair tangled
As if by wind, the mouth
Open to speak, to say
Eye's leak, the open ear.

When the storms start
And swell the waters
Behind the dam, the stones
May well part, and in their dark canoes
The dead will sweep down river.

What is King Canute's surprise
Beside this? The dead
Are touring the day.

Two Secret Photographs

I. Scene
Islands, clipped and bound,
Sea stapled, crisp,
Landscapes like lettuce,
Empty and involved, alive.

Only on a visit, the hesitant shoe,
First on sand, then pines, stone.

Vivid, the eye strains for control,
Inclined for shadows, lost in sun,
Easy to remember, harder to see,
West and east, the south, south.

II. Scheme
Inside the camera: I

Look like clouds, opaque,
Obscure, locked like an opal,
Valuable as old china,
Entire, a house in cedars.

You are curved in woods,
Oak perhaps, or slick elm,
Unique: the camera in sight.

Luke XXIII

(After the Spanish of Jorge Luis Borges)

Nameless by time, defaced,
No more aware of mercy
Than any sentenced thief,
He heard, hung on death's tree,
The crowd's remark: how God
Sagged like fruit
On the next warped branch.

Said, darkly, "Lord,
Remember me
When you come into your own."

And the voice beyond knowing,
Judge of us all, took him in.

The terrible cross
Stained with paradise.

Pride remembers the two,
A memory stretched up to the sun.

And you know, good friend, the candor
Of this friend of Christ, his simple request
Called through the torture's shame,
Its quick result.

Know, too, how that same innocence
Has thrown you more than once to sin,
To the accidents of blood, of death.

Les Ombres Artificielles

Homage to Alain Robbe-Grillet

De nouveau la scène est vide.

The light as diffuse and bright
As light, a corridor marked

By the interruption of doors,
Of the knobs of doors,
Each one as bright and precise
As light, one window
At the far end of the corridor,
The quick stutter of doors.

The light as diffuse and dim
As light, a corridor blurred
By the interruption of doors,
Of the knobs of doors,
Each one as dim and precise
As light, one window
At the far end of the corridor,
The dull progression of doors.

The light as acute and bright
As light, a corridor cut
By the interruption of doors,
Of the knobs of doors,
Each one as bright and approximate
As light, one window
At the far end of the corridor,
The deadly accuracy of doors.

Once more the scene is empty.

The Other Tiger

(After the Spanish of Jorge Luis Borges)

*"And the craft that createth a semblance, and fails of the heart's
desire;
And the toil that each dawning quickens and the task that is
never done,
And the heart that longeth ever, nor will look to the deed that
is won."*

Reading Morris, you think of a tiger,
The living coal of fire. The dark library
Expands, large and alive, larger, the shelves
Push back; excessive, innocent, tawny and tangerine,
The tiger, blooded and new, will walk

Through its jungle, will sink its tracks
In the river's wet bank, a river whose name
It will not know (a world and moment
Without name or time), will walk wild ways,
Will scent in the woven wind sweet dawn and deer.
In the partings of the bamboo you discover
The sharp stripes of its hair, feel
The bones hard through the hot hide.
A world curves, water and sand, in vain;
In the lost south, South America,
You dream the tiger you trace,
"O tiger on the banks of the Ganges."

The afternoon spreads like a soul,
Your soul as you reflect that the tiger
To whom you just spoke in this poem
Is only symbols and shadows, memories
From the encyclopedia, literary turns,
No deadly tiger, no fatal jewel
Under the Sumatran sun, moon of Bengal,
A round of love and laziness and death.
You have set against this symbolic beast
The real thing, the tiger of warm blood,
Hungry for buffalo, heedless of horn,
That stretches in the high grass today,
The third of August, 1959 (and today,
20th of March, 1970), and today, a shadow at rest,
Still and quiet by the act of its naming,
Already the fiction of your thought,
No living tiger breathing the air of the earth.

We shall search out a third tiger:
Like the others stretched out in this poem,
The form of our dreaming, shape of our words,
Man-made, spineless, not the quick tiger
That knows and stalks the days beyond all myth.
What drives us from the grasses into the trees,
Drives us to this hunt, this empty hunt,
Ancient and absurd? We press on, blind
In the late afternoon, hunting the other tiger,
The one who is never in a poem.

✌

Another Tiger

Homage to Jorge Luis Borges

In Buenos Aires, the first tiger:
Delicate in the river mud,
Marking a sharp line
On the border
Of land and water.

We know the river's name,
More than the tiger knows.

Still he walks there
By the river.

He does not stop to drink.

The second tiger:
A real one, hungry and hot,
This one in India
After buffalo.

It hangs soon in the rooms of your mind
However,
Tanned in the heat of your name.

Another tiger:

A jaguar perhaps, circles within circles
On its tawny hide, hung in a tree
Over the trail.

The sun conspires with the leaves
To hide him from your eyes.

You return to Buenos Aires,
To the library by the silver river.

Tigers and tigers haunt its stacks.

The jaguar licks its fur
And lolls in the sheltering leaves.

Three Places

for Lew

1.

Siphoned, the light
This afternoon is as gray
As dawn, this dawn
Leaking through the trees
In Pennsylvania (you could hear it
Spilling through birds),
Still on the flat layers of stone
Half buried in pine needles.

And now with the day half done
You are watching a windmill turn
Against clouds, waiting for sunset,
Wondering at rain.

2.

Fetid, this wet cellar:
The dirt of one wall communes
With the rushing of rain.
You strain at the windows,
Your lungs taut with coal dust,
Hold yourself closer.
The dry bulb in the ceiling
Drowns in the smell of the rain.

Not so this attic
Where the wood shatters
To the crack of your heels,
And the dust is as still
As your breath, held close,
The air dry and odorless,
The sunlight wrinkling
Through the windows
Like a bird weary
From thrashing at the glass.

3.
Flow: a high wind
Across Lancaster County
Touched with gulls,
With echoes of ocean,
Hints of salt.

You watch
The waterwheel
Dazzle the stream.

The water is as cold,
As clean as the white clouds,
As the sparrows, alert
In the whitewashed tree.

Three small girls
Are too shy to speak;
They flap like blue flags.

The noon sun
Sets you in a shadowy pool,
No larger when you stand.

The soil is warm and broken;
The wind slides the new grass
Toward you. It never arrives.

Upstream, a horse noses the water;
Foam breaks out from his touch,
A finger of air gloved in water.

Blind Pew

(After the Spanish of Jorge Luis Borges)

> *And may I
> And all my pirates share the grave
> Where these and their creations lie!*
> —R. L. Stevenson

Stranded from the sea, cut off
From war (both packed along,
Long lost, by love), the pirate

Winds the ways of England, blind
As dirt.

Barked at by farm dogs, dogged
By roving boys, he sleeps a sleep
Sickly and sour in the roots
Of hedges, ditches by a road, black
In the dirt.

He knows far golden beaches (sand
Covers his treasure's gold), knows
Exactly; he eases his life
In the sand.

You, too, know a beach of gold,
Far beach, your treasure buried,
Mapped:
          Death—crowded, vast, vague
As sand.

❧

Welcome

for Dorothy and Mimi

Like a patched banner, small holes
Cut like half-hearted moons
For the wind, hanging boldly
Where your open car might pass.

Like a handshake at the door
Where you are the 2,000[th] one
In, and the photograph that follows.
In the newspaper, your curious smile
Surrounded by grins.

Like a pot of bright petals,
Stems and fat leaves, a release
Of hot balloons, a key tucked
Under the doormat, a message
From the new management,
Red ribbons, an open window.

Like the wave of the stout cop
Who passes you through

And around back where you enter
An unmarked and knobless door.

Like a shower of paper tape,
Torn newspapers, envelopes
And tidy memos from the boss
Marked URGENT, shredding
The sunlight on the avenue.

Like the echoes of dogs
Passing your passing up the street
On a night when the moon is full
And the puddles on the pavement
Shine like the eyes of dogs.

Like proffered paws, curtsies,
Hard handshakes, stiff handshakes,
Limp handshakes, hugs, quick kisses,
Longer kisses, disturbing kisses,
Stares, blushes, disappearances,
Fatted calves, bottles, bottles,
Hearty waves, large cigars, winks,
Fireworks, salutes, demonstrations,
Inspections, and badges:

Boxes of new badges, round
And perfectly white with red letters
Reading: HELLO. Reading: WELCOME.
Reading: WHAT'S YOUR NAME?
Reading: THIS TIME
YOU'VE REALLY COME TO STAY.

Map

But, even with imaginary places, he will
do well in the beginning to provide
a map. As he studies it, relations
will appear that he had not thought upon.
        —R. L. Stevenson

A map with a scale of 3 English miles
Held against the sea by mermaids,

Their breasts salty and bare,
Their hair slick as a seal:

Fish lie on the waves, mouths
Open like gills to the air,
As birds burst from the sea,
Row into the air and fly.

The land is broken by swamps
And graves (the bones' slow rot
In the damp, loose earth). South
Of the island there is foul ground,
Too, where rocks break the water
Like hungry fish, like birds.
A strong tide sucks the western shore.

The ship lies in 10 fathoms
Off the narrow spit
Where white rock stands
Like a raw statue. Gulls
Swing out from the stone
Like flat rocks skipping
Low across the water
And circle the masts,
Crying like fish on the waves,
Crying like mermaids at night.

Lines solid and broken
Sweep out from the compass
Like broken glass, slice
Through the water
And under the land,
Tie sea and soil together
Like a spyglass swung slowly
From west to north to east.

The moon draws at the tide.
Skeletons of fish slide
On the sand to the roots of trees.
Gulls mutter in their sleep
And dream of the rising sea.
The mermaids hold against the tide,
Their tails splashing in the moon,
A scale of 3 English miles.

A World

El anverso y el reverso de esta moneda
son, par Dios, iguales.

Borges speaks of a world
Of bored barbarity, of monotonous
Savagery, of dull cruelty.

True enough.

He continues
But the world remains.

A leg breaks lazily,
Splitting the long way
Like the branch of a walnut
With the weight of ice.

In the dark building
They tie you to a chair
And edge you, straining,
To the edge of the stairs.

The long rows blur
To a grey serpent, sliding
Crookedly across the mud,
The chains lashing
Like ground teeth,
Sharp as your fear,
The water of your nerve.

The prevalence of blood,
Spreading on the highway,
Pooling in the sour cellar,
Draining under the locked door,
A heart pumps wildly
Into the stained air.

Words that strike
Like shaggy spears, like stones,
Like short, honed swords,
The quiet words that stick

In the comfortable air
Like clumsy darts.

The eyes of animals swell
In their heads, their lips
Tug nervously back, hackles
Stiff as dry blood. A wind
Rises and clatters the dark wood.
Grasses snarl in the clearing.
Rain stings like lead pellets.
The walls of the house strain
Like foundering ships.

Your side cracked like a husk,
Jesus, sprayed the soldier's
Face with blood and water:

Cracked like graves
With the bodies of waking saints,
Like rent garments,
Like the rotten temple wall:

Cracked like dry skin,
Dry dirt around the base
Of the skull:

Cracked like a caul,
Like the sweet taste
Of walnuts, of water,
Cracked like parting waters,
Like the scales of a new bud
Hot in the darkened air.

Wheel

Siempre se pierde lo esencial.

Perhaps carved in stone,
Its spokes rigid as the four fixed signs
Of the zodiac, on the chariot
Of an Assyrian king, his ridged beard
Formal as the spokes, or of a pharoah
Drawn by lean horses, their front feet

Multiplied by two, by four,
Carved in the air,
In all their hurry, in stone.

Or in silver on film,
Spinning backwards as the coach
Picks up speed, spilling dust
Down the center of town,
Slowing down and reversing
Like an electric fan
On a gusty day, stopping
In the dust that rises and falls
Like shadows on film in silver.

Or a captain lashed in a storm,
Hung on the rungs like a side of beef,
His daughter, salty and stiff,
Tied to the broken mast, the rudder
Beating the waves to the consistency
Of foam, of the little girl's hair
Spun out like frayed canvas,
Of the smoking sea in a storm.

Borges speaks of a circular delirium,
Of an encompassing circle, of circular
Ruins, of the zero, the cipher, coin
Like a crystal egg, cat's eye.

The harsh jackel's head of Anubis
Grins like a dog over a gnawed bone,
Its spine shivered with selfish hair.
The calm face of the sphinx
Is a mirror to the empty air.

If fortune is a wheel,
What is a wheel?

Rain

(*After the Spanish of Jorge Luis Borges*)

The afternoon produces a rain.

It also falls in the past.

You hear it. You remember the day
You first saw the color of a rose,
Saw the flower (you knew the name).

This rain closes the window,
But it opens tiny lenses in the screen
Of the room you knew, slicks the plums
On a bent tree that is no more.

This wet afternoon brings you the sound
You have been listening for:

Your father's voice, alive in the rain.

Three Friends

1. Dufy

Dufy's head settles securely in his collar.
Nature, he said, is only an hypothesis.
His striped tie signifies no school.

Dufy in a small white car in 1929:
He looks out of the rear window
Over the fat spare tire.
He misses, then, the large green car
Just ahead, and the casino at Nice,
But he sees a blue bush, a green bush,
Someone in blue making a blue sketch.

In 1925 while they are playing jazz,
Dufy sees Helene's arm, poised
Like an epaulet on Paul's shoulder.

It is necessary, he said, to create
A world of things that one does not see.

The smoke of the blue train is as blue
As grass. My favorite nude is there.
Dufy has just stepped back for a look,
Only a band of blue on his canvas.
The sun in the green sky is as warm
On her skin as Dufy's hand
If he were there.

Like music or a poem, he said, art
Is a creation. Dufy hums the Mozart blues.

2. Léger

Léger's cap is a little large.
Machine made, it fits him
Like a halo or a glove.

Léger watches a building
Sprout from the earth
Like a locust, a weed
At first, wooding upward,
A tall tree, bending
In high winds, blooming.

Léger knows who made each machine
And each machinist.

On a picnic, he tinkers
With the motor of the odd car
While we touch each other
With the delicacy of mechanics.
The dog takes his ease
In the shade of Léger's coat,
Hung like a blossom on the tree.

Léger sees the city,
How buildings reflect
The angles of builders,
How smoke balloons
Over an engine,
How that man is constructed
Like a fine machine.

To see, hear, and touch,
Léger said, a multitude
Of things. He grins
Like a clown with a banjo.
He doffs his hat

With happy precision,
Like a flower
Wound up with keys.

3. Turner

Turner's gaze is steady.
You want to turn away,
Turn it off like a light.

To an open eye, the elements
Fuse, fire, water and air
As parliament burns in oil,
The sun writhing like a water snake
As the sun sets in the Thames,
Earth, air, fire and water one
As parliament burns in watercolor,
To Turner's open eye.

Turner leans from the railway coach,
His head blurred in the fast rain,
Only a shower in a blue sky,
And he sees a boat on the river,
Picnickers, the black smokestack
And the black smoke sliding
Down the traincars in the rain.

I did not paint it to be understood,
Turner said, but I wished to show
What such a scene was like.

Turner watches a German mountain
Paint itself with the sunset,
Pale in the evening air
Across the fading water. He sees
How even a sea monster is swallowed
By sunrise, how light ages and changes,
How the shape of the world
Is the shape of an eye.

Homage to Henry Green

It was no more or less, really,
Than we had expected:
Rose after rose after rose

Beyond a roadway asphalted blue,
The blood colored brick,
The young man in pink tweeds;

Or the nervous butler
With two very different eyes.

It is all in a manner of seeing.

He sees music like maids
In a ballroom. He sees
Fear like a dead pigeon.
He sees walls split like chestnuts
In the fire and burn the blue streets.

And he knows the limits of love:
Desire, memory, an end like suttee.

The afternoon slows silently
Into evening like music,
Like fear, like fire.

His eyes are warm
Like coals in a grate.
He sees the room sway
To the music of the fire.
He is safe and sure
In the boundaries of love.

No more, no less, really,
Than we had expected.

Three Books from Babel

The Combed Thunderclap
A tooth once seen
Grows like a fang,
A claw, a nail, a bolt,
A row of teeth, a comb,
A noise of teeth,
The thunderbolt.

The Plaster Cramp
A caught curve,
Crook, flat ring,

The circle spreads
As in a pond
Indefinitely.

Axaxaxas Mlö
Unknown,
The error of a circle,
Spread of the compass,
Odd, awkward, like an egg,
Like a word caught on the teeth.

❧

Argumentum Ornithologicum
(After the Spanish of Jorge Luis Borges)

Close your eyes. You see
A flock of birds. Flown
Quicker than you can draw
A bead. How many birds?

You could not count. No
Count could be so sudden.
And suddenly the existence
Of God is at hand. So:

If God is, God knows
The number of birds
You saw. If God is not,
The birds remain a flock.

Let's say you saw more
Than one bird, saw less
Than ten, a number, then,
Between one and ten.

And let's allow Borges
To eliminate *nueve*,
Ocho, siete, seis, cinco,
Cuatro, tres or *dos.*

Now you: a number between
One and ten, not nine,
Nor eight, six, seven,
Five, three or four or two.

An integer, whole number,
That number, even or odd,
Is beyond you, me or Borges,
Ergo, the existence of God.

New Anger

It worries you as you
Would worry a wart,
A dried tongue of cuticle.

You think of muscle,
Knots, teeth, thumbs.
Your knees ache.

You dream of knuckles
And glass, fresh air,
The salt and water of blood.

You swallow back the burn
Of your stomach, expect
Your throat to open

As you stare at the mirror,
Explode like a rotted can,
Flanges as black as poison.

You wish you could cough
It up on the floor, mop
It into a pail like jelly.

You know the rasp
Of your bones, why only
The dead are free from sin.

America Is Darken'd

Washington, Franklin, Paine & Warren, Gates, Hancock &
Green
          —William Blake

"Now, my dear friend, what is our plan?"
Cornwallis wrote to Phillips,

Already tired of Greene and Guilford,
Soon to leave with no reply
For Yorktown and Washington,
De Rochambeau and Comte de Grasse.

How could he know how Washington
Burned in the imagination of Blake,
How red hairy Orc squeezes out of earth
Like a tough vine to bloom in Yorktown?

Children, their clothes shed
Like worn skin, ride the tamed serpent,
As relaxed as fat lambs.

The *Terrible* blazes off Cape Charles.
Pale women burn in the flames, swell
Like new grapes on the vine, spread
Their legs and fly like smoke
Across Cape Charles, across Yorktown,
Darkening the blue mountains,
The dim midwest, the Rockies
Where the sun burns down like a pyre,
Like a ship hissing down in salt water.

What could Cornwallis do?
He and his armies fared better
In India where the fire was unreal,
Where elephants kneeled on command,
Where dark men were used to Juggernaut
And could agree to the benefits of the wheel.

Lord North cried, "O God! It is all over!"

In America, Blake's dream burns on.
The smoke stings the eye to tears.
A lizard tongues insects in the scorched air.
Bolts and hinges are melted.
Snakes hiss from every hip and thigh.

Blake wove his FINISH in thorns
With blooms as hot as coals. Trees
Clutch each other like lust. Men
Clutch the earth and bloom like fruitful trees.
The eye ignites to see. The hand holds.
Blake's dream burns on.

Kite

for Judy

A kite holds in the April air
So steady a crossbow's bolt
Could trace the string
Straight to its crossed sticks.

You approve what Hammett
Said, that things belong
To those who want them most.

The kite climbs and hovers
In the steady air like a kite,
One of the "hawks of southern
Distribution," shaped like a falcon,
Wings sharp as the bolt of a crossbow,
Flat as a magpie in the April sky.

You are focussed in the steady light
So sharply the day centers on you.
The kite string unwinds like film.
The bright sun clicks like a shutter.

The kite opens like a light sail
In a light wind, bounces once
Like a note, crosses
The sun like a wink.

The day belongs to you to give
Or save. The kite steadies
The April air. The sun centers
Like a kite across the day,
Like the sharp pupil in the iris
Of the sky, blue as the focus
Of an open eye.

❧

Last Flight

He was flying like a bird,
and he went down in flames.
   —John O'Hara

"No, you can't talk to him.
He's right here,
But he's dead." Both feet
Off the icy road at last.

Waiting for winter,
You disliked the summer air,
Smooth as water, clear
As glass. You knew the way
From day to day.

Winter came
And spring, eggy weather,
High winds, late frost,
Ice, not much sunlight,
Snow blowing across Pennsylvania
All April.

But your heart jolted up
Like something in May,
One last flight, abrupt,
You soloed like a pro.

And came to light.

We wonder what is next.
You know.

❧

A Yellow Rose

(After the Spanish of Jorge Luis Borges)

Laid out in bed, near
The end, the old writer,
This new Homer, new Dante,

His room over a garden,
Marble, laurels, step after step,
Down to a pool doubling the day,
The laurels, the marble,
Step after step, he sees:

A yellow rose.

The woman has placed it
In his goblet by the bed.

He speaks his piece,
Lines as smooth and familiar
As the carved posts of the bed:
Porpora de'giardin, pompa de'prati,
gemma di primavera, occhio d'aprile . . .

He sees it:

A yellow rose, his eye edenic,
Open as Adam's,
A yellow rose.

His words do not hold it
Like a goblet. It is itself.
We may, he sees, allude to a rose
Or name a rose. We may, he knows,
Never say a rose at all.

The gold of his books on the shelf
Glows like a mirror. They are
No mirror, he sees, to the world.
They are only another item in it.

This light found Giambattista Marino
Like a knife before he died.

Perhaps it opened Homer's eyes
As well, was like a pinpoint small
As it is bright to Dante, too.

♾

Hats

Annie appears, arrayed
In an amazing assortment
Of hats.

They stagger above her
Like a happy drunk
Looking for the familiar lamppost.

What a strange creature,
The Martian must think,
Taking a quick snap
From the step of his lander,
I hope this shot comes out.

All of my friends
Are astounded. They
Applaud, not really knowing
What is expected of them.
As always, they have done
The right thing.

Her walk is a dance
Taller than telephone poles.
Birds light lightly
On the brims.

The grass is alert
Underfoot for droppings.
Three small hats do fall:
The Sudanese felt tarboosh
And the two York Harbor
Paper fireman's hats.
They bounce like dervishes,
Like water drops on a hot roof.

What a strange creature,
You must think. So do I.
Odd that she should prove
So lovely. Odder still
How her eyes are friendly
Like the tracks of birds,

How her hands are safe
As the eyelids of birds.

The Mining of Soapstone

The stone is as soft as soap,
You carve your name slowly
And the name, like soap, slips away,
Talc rock, steatite, so soft
You can cut it with your knife,
Slips away, blue, green,
Under the blade like sea shavings,
Swallows light in your palm, dark green, blue.

The mine grounds a hillside:
You have leaned around the road
That curves through pine woods
And elm high above, but here
The dark cut opens beyond
The narrow stream, fringed with soapwort
And tattered sunflowers.

At sea, off Tobago, swimming,
You are soft as soap, the salt
Crusts your skin, stings like the brush
Of rays sliding through the soapfish,
The sunfish, the air hot and buggy,
Fish eyes like buttons of soapberries,
Red as soapbark or the roots of soapwort,
The dark water still through the light
Swimming on the surface, spilling
Underwater like a Man-of-War.

The narrow tracks swerve once
And descend, the wood pitted
And harsh against the slick walls,
As ahead, down, beneath, you hear
The soft picking of blades into soapstone.

Your ears hover like gnats,
You are seasick below sea level,
The tracks coil like fish,

The ground slips away underfoot,
Your lips pucker for air,
Alone in blue green soapstone
You swim in a film of silence
You can cut with your knife.

The Study of Ecology

The examination of leaves:

Thoreau saw the tree,
The veins against sunlight,
Also looked at his hand—
Branching, veined, barked,
The fine black hairs
That need sunlight to be seen,
Lines, branches, the universal M,
Cain's mark.

Raise your hand, hold it,
Know the stilling of winter,
And when you grow tired, forget
And let it fall, the flow
Of new springs.

You rub your eyes,
Bone, skin on water,
You see heavens, stars,
Fires, fire.

Leaves riddle with sunlight
The ground, the grass,
Your hand, holding sunlight,
Leaves of shadow, of air.

More Tigers, Dreamtigers

(After the Spanish of Jorge Luis Borges)

*We might contrive a very poetical and very
suggestive . . . philosophy, by supposing that
the virtuous live while the wicked suffer*

31

As a boy you lived tigers,
Asiatic tigers, royal and aloof,
In zoos, in books, approached
By cautious elephants with slit ears,
Castled with warriors.

You still remember them every one:
They replace days, faces, the smiles of women.

And they return nightly in the shadows
Of your dreams.

You are sleeping; a dream leads you astray.
You know you are dreaming. You think:
I am dreaming, a pure diversion of my will.
You hold power without limits.
You will cause a tiger to be.

Good bungler, no tiger appears.
Oh, a tiger does arrive, a stuffed tiger,
Or a gentle one, one with too long a tail
Or brown eyes, one as large as an elephant,
A flash of fur in the leaves, no danger,
A tiger that wags its tail and barks,
Or sings on a limb like a small yellow bird.

More News

I was heart and soul involved in
everything that happened; how, then,
can I deal with it objectively, or with
the hidden significance behind it?
            —Gamal Abdul Nasser

It is autumn.
A news is pressing.

Amber saps slide out of the trees
Like hurt sunlight.
Weathers waver.

A news is pressing.
Across the ocean they bury the dead.
They bury the dead next door.
The ground cracks like bark.
Your shadow moves strangely.
You are closer to earth
As the air disappears.

A Tiger You May Have Missed

A tiger a rapt and surrounded overcoat securely arranged
with spots old enough to be thought useful and witty
quite witty in a secret and in a blinding flurry.
      —Gertrude Stein

This one as simple as a blanket,
Worn, warm, cut out of words
Like pinks and cool red roses.

What happened: a tiger in alphabets,
Arranged securely, safe as bars,
An old tiger put out on view,
Open as an eye to the eye.

A tiger, bluntly put, placed,
Set, practical and sure,
But your eye still wraps itself
In awe, in sharp surprise.

Then the tiger, hermetic, secret,
Blends in, disappears in lines,
In spots, in flurries of the eye,
Sudden, deadly, silent,
Lost to your thought, wound
In your eye, invisible in words.

You start again, again
The tiger disappears; again,
Again. But he grows familiar,

You know his trick and watch
Him go, like a blanket wearing out,
An overcoat, a shoe, a rose,
A tiger by the river, in the zoo.

Bela Lugosi: Three Lines

1. 1930
To be dead, to be really dead,
That must be glorious.
But you cried like a man undone
When the stake broke in:
The truth of Dracula
In that last sound, off camera,
Somewhere to the right of focus.

2. 1933
A simpler truth: *Death*
Is always very close.
In the liver, the heart,
The room across the hall,
The food in the jar,
The unexpected call
Late at night.

3. 1934
Master of old fly eaters,
King of the rats, batwing
And red eye, you knew
The lesson of the veins,
The secrets of circulation.
Any way you cut it,
It was always the same:
Supernatural, perhaps.
Baloney, perhaps not.

Epilogue

(After the Spanish of Jorge Luis Borges)

The exchange which is fanciful and righteous
and mingled is in the author mostly in the piece.
　　—Gertrude Stein

You set out to shape a world.
Years pass: stones, wind in grass,
Mountains, the echoes of bays,
Waves, the stirring of tides,
Kingdoms, republics, states
Of the mind, old walls and scrolls,
Ships and sailors, sheets and sails,
Fishes, finny and fast, and sharks,
Rooms, closets, the cellar stairs,
Instruments and tools, knives, stars,
Horses and horsemen, women, men.

And then at the end, before you die,
You examine the maze of careful lines
To find there a face, wearing
And worn, warm as worn stone,
A face you know: your own.

Construction

It seems that the human mind has first to construct
forms independently before we can find them in things.
　　—Albert Einstein

Vladimir Tatlin's demand:
Real materials in real space,

Solid and silent, an art of iron,
Of concrete, cut wood and glass.

A response: to say as you see,
Words set firm like a jaw.

The descent into silence. An ascent.
You breathe as you sleep, you circulate.

To say as you see. To see as by stop-action,
Clouds coil overhead, the passage of days,

Trees bend by the side of the road
Like tires on a curve, plants uncurl,

How the world dissolves in the water of the eye:
The illusion speed produces. The reality of speed.

A result: to see as you say,
As gravity may bend a ray of light.

To say the earth's center is of fire:
Life leaps from the soil like sun flares.

To see the world made true,
An art of rocks and stones and trees,

Real materials in real space,
L'esthétique de la vitesse.

Three More Friends

1. Ryder
It is hard to see Ryder sometimes
For the light, solid as trees,
It breaks through his worried eyes
And the orchard turns to light,
You could touch it, squeezed out
As from a tube, lighter than the eye
Recalls, cracking under the strain,
Better than nature, Ryder said,
The thrill of a new creation.

Ryder is a young man in a field,
Like a colt let loose, he said,
Learning to see how a field
Is a fold of the sky, with no details
To vex the eye, earth and leaves
And sky. He bellowed for joy.

Ryder in the Forest of Arden
Is as hard to see as lovers,
The trees like clouds, the clouds
Leaning on the air like trees,
And Ryder watches the day pass
In his eyes, trying to find, he said,
Something out there beyond the place
On which I have a footing.

Ryder at sea, Ryder at morning,
Ryder dreaming the history of the mind,
The witches lost in a shadow,
The moon burning like the point of a match
Through paper, the clouds singed,
The witches lost in shadow,
The sails of ships shaping the air
Like pyramids or tornadoes,
And Christ glows like a moon or a sun.

There is surprise in Ryder's face
When he looks at you, or recognition,
And you see shadows in his eyes
And a light as solid as trees.

2. Homer

He is as solid as a businessman,
His collar etches his neck like acid,
A flower shedding in his buttonhole,
Homer, with a moustache like a brush,
Sprayed out and stiff, scrawled.

But a wave kisses the moon
And you know what it is to live
In water, or light as air on rapids,
Or broken as sand on a beach.
Just *look* at it! Homer said,
And color washes the eye like a dawn,
Or air, or sea water that scalds.

Homer at Prouts Neck,
Buttoned up, stiff as an easel,
Will not meet your eye,
But the Gulf Stream cracks
Over his shoulder, like a pioneer
He knows the ax must break a tree

Before we learn the lesson of light,
Like a fisherman, he knows
The rhythms of water, the shattering
Of moonlight on the shore,
The uses of calm and of silence.

What I remember best, Homer said,
Is the smell of paint, his hand
Moves like a shark or a whip,
His eyes like a knife, cutting away,
Narrow as an oriental's, moving
Like palm leaves in a hot wind,
Fill my pipe for me, he said,
His eyes like a fox in deep snow,
His hand steady as a crow,
I'm too busy to stop.

3. Hopper

At night the electric light
Makes new shadows and new spaces,
Echoes in the street,
Or in a dark theater in 1939
Where Hopper is watching *Dark Victory*
It separates you from the shadow
And holds you like a still life,
Pensive, alone, alive.

What I wanted to do, Hopper said,
Was to paint sunlight on the side
Of a house, sunlight seen solid,
Sunlight on white walls, on windows,
On a white fence, sunlight
In brick shadows, on brick walls,
Sunlight as blue as an ocean,
As brown as a roof, as solid as sand.

You meet him in Chicago,
Or early Sunday morning in New York,
He is alone on Manhattan Bridge
Or having coffee late at night,
He knows the democracy of light,
Light on a bridge in Manhattan,
Or a bridge breaking pine woods,
On a house by the railroad,

The equality of trees and wood siding,
Light on a lighthouse, or light
On the shoulders of a friend.

Hopper's face is like windows,
You see yourself or a landscape,
The angles of stonework and steel,
The subtleties of water,
The energy of oil, Hopper's face
Is like sunlight, alone and alive.

Waking Up

*And I perceived, suddenly, that the dull melancholy
of half a year was lifted from my mind.*
    —H. G. Wells

The way the room takes shape,
Pale and shallow, and the clock's face
Damps down like the stars. You open
Slowly, like mist over water.

The pupils of your eyes are black,
Are round and deep as wells.
You see the branches of trees
In the window, the dimmest of shadows
Spilling back from the trees,
The dew heavy as sea water
On the shadowy, flat grass.

The day deepens like poured water.
The leaves of the trees are red
And dry green, are light as the air.
A blue feather dries on the grass.

You are moving like oil on water,
The muscles of your arms electric
And sharp, your hands open and moving.
Your skull cracks like a shell.
Something stirs in the wells of your eyes.

The air deepens and wavers
Like sunlight through water.
You are shiny and plastic,

Like the new leaf of a plant.
The pupils of your eyes tighten
The sunlight. They hold it.

You are open like a window,
Trim as copper screening
In the clear autumn air.
You are moving like shadows
Over the opening grass.
You are rising like water
In the dry autumn air.

❧

She

(After the English of Jorge Luis Borges)

> *In town or field, or by the insatiate sea,*
> *Men brood on buried loves, and unforgot. . . .*
> —H. Rider Haggard

You want her.
You have little to offer:

Your hour under the moon,
The blue asphalt like steel,
The memory you hold of a smile,
Caught like silver in your eye,
A touch of fingers, her hand
Held out from the window
As she leaves (the last time).

A past: dead men, ghosts,
An odor of verbena, "dying thunder of hooves,"
The charge of three hundred men in Peru,
Your father's father wrapped in the hide of a cow,
A soldier shot at Gettysburg,
Caught among boulders, his leg stiff as leather,
The knife his son fashioned,
Touched now with rust, sharp as an eye.

The expression of your books,
The books themselves, green, orange, gold,
The paper stiff as a knee.

Your loyalty
And the fact of your betrayals.

Yourself, the smile no mirror shows,
Safe from time, from joy, from pain.

A glimpse of a yellow rose
In a goblet by a bed.

Your theories of her:
News that opens like a knife, a window,
Authentic and surprising news.

The loneliness that wakes you late and lonely,
The hunger that wakes you,
The lure of uncertainty, danger,
The possibility of defeat.

Homage to Eric Ambler

Like water oiling the bristled piles,
Rust on a freighter's plates,
Moving like shadows along the dockside,
The thin scratch of a phonograph,
The needle scraping like wool on chafed skin,
The touch of a hand for only a moment,
An echo, an echo, an echo like water.

You stand on the balcony with a slim cigar,
You know too much, your eyes are heavy with it,
You are in fog leaning like a streetlamp,
Like a street, wet and electric,
Aware of common danger, a passage as of arms,
A state of continuing siege, your eyes are heavy,
Like smoke, like fog, like the roll of waters.

The light crackles down mountain walls
So that your hair stands on end, you tighten,
The darkness flees into alleyways,
Under trees, slips under passing cars,
You are tense as a lit fuse, sparks,
A hiss of nerves, you strike a match
With a scrape like needles on the stone wall.

But you have solved it, working alone,
Working with others and no loss of self-respect,
Cracked it like a simple code, notes of a song,
You feel the hand that holds hard, that grips,
Your eyes as narrow as the iris of a lens,
You say the word, the words, like the light
That spreads on water, you see the broken day:

You write it on the walls.

March Again

*The stable universe is slipping away
from under us.*
—A. N. Whitehead

How the light returns to you,
How even the gray bark of trees
Seems to shed light and the ground
Is as bright and as fluid as air.
How your skin opens like an eye:
You are warm as glass, as clear.

In the evening it snows
And the wind rattles the roof
Like knuckles or bullets,
The curtains puff away
From the closed windows.
You hold to the lamp's circle,
Well away from the wall.
Only blood moves through you
Like light through fog,
You close your eyes
And the room silently moves.

In the morning the wind sharpens
The pond to blades, to light,
Wave on wave on wave.
You grow dizzy and each step
Is like walking on water,
Is like walking on knives.
The wind is around you like a wall.

How you are stirring like a bulb
In soil, you open like an eye,
The lids curled back like lips
In a snarl, how you follow
The shadows of birds, a tatter
As of discarded paper or shavings,
How the day stretches like dogs
And the shadows shrink in the grass.

Christ could have swum away
From the cross on air,
But he chose to be nailed
To the ground. You grow dizzy
And each step is like walking
On water, is like walking on knives.
The ground sheds light like a lamp.
The wind rattles the trees like bones.
Only blood calls you to move
Well away from the walls.

The House We Live In

for John and Elizabeth Rodenbeck

The house in which we live:

First past the door you must face
The gorilla (no real test)
Or the grinning dog.
The mirror holds you
Like a surprise.

And then the open doors.

A room of walls:
The whale swimming in its sea of mystic fire,
Two small girls (you remember them)
Lit on a haymow in the bundled field,
The machine is red, the sun yellow and round,
The lost circus rider,
The puzzled horse, a phoenix in gold,
A nervous face by Jacques Villon,
And the wild buffalo hot and new as skin.

43

Other rooms:
The blue one where Annie works,
The dining room with its blue Arabic plate,
The green kitchen where plants thrive
(And white flies),
The red room where you are always welcome.

And windows:
The grass begins to breathe this month
(April) sliced with early onions,
Trees blossom, the air sweetens
With honeysuckle as the creek slides
Below us clear as old memories
(Ours, yours, Max's memory of the car,
Friedl's of the mosques in Devon).

Annie is opening the door
And the day ambles in, shaking itself
And stretching. She examines the road.
She is looking for you.

You come too.

Anniversary

How six years can slip by
Like the stammer of an eye
And fill the air like life:

1. Sugar
Sugar, the spiral in a cup,
Carbon, hydrogen, oxygen,
The crystallization of air,
Hard life, the bitter, the sweet.

A gift of sugar:
Light sprinkling the bay water
Like sugar, our eyes as tight
As a squeeze. We are on the dock,
Docked as waves slap the wood
And gulls squall and tumble overhead.
There is a breeze, and it is June.
Your hair in this clear light

Is like sunlight sprinkled on waves,
Or crystals catching the air.

Cane sugar, beet sugar, maple sugar,
Sugar extracted in mills or drawn
From the tree with a wooden spile,
Diffused, evaporated, crystallized,
A sludge of molasses, sugar, sugar.

A gift of sugar:
It will dissolve in rain
Or brown and smear in fire,
It is like a kiss (quickly)
Or perhaps the touch of a sleeve,
Too sweet to taste long
And bitter, too, gone with a brush
Of the hand or a puff of fresh air,
It is like eyes meeting, a glance
And then a glance away,
You taste it on your lips
For a second, you remember it
For years.

2. Candy
Boiled sugar or molasses, candy, toffee,
Drawn out in long loops, viscous and heavy,
Like afternoons in summer when you are slow,
When you hold yourself in a long embrace
And will not go or do.

A gift of candy:
You are hot and naked from the bath,
Even the air is wet and heavy,
You are shining and hot
And you move like steam.
You turn inward like the slow suck
Of the drain, turning back like a clock.
You think of broad leaves after rain,
Of clean air, of skin soft and humid.
Your arms are open and sweet
Like candy, or sunsets in summer.

Candy and chocolate, jellies and jams,
With fruit, wrapped in gold foil
Or red and white wrappers, candies in bins

45

Behind glass, a handful of candy, a fist,
The slow warm spread of blood in an embrace.

A gift of candy:
It is a gift of time.

3. Iron

Or iron, elemental, ductile,
Tenacious. A day like iron
With high white clouds, pure iron,
A breeze that cools like the touch of iron,
The sun hot as white hot stones
Or the red touch of heated iron.
You are standing alone by running water
As green leaves whistle in your ears,
And you see water and wet earth,
Air that moves and holds, the fire
Of blood and sun. Time moves, time holds.
A day as rare as native iron.

A gift of iron:
The pressure of a hand on your shoulder,
So hard the grip that you breathe deeper,
Hold yourself tense as a rabbit or a match,
Focus all color into muscle and nerve.
Or the smooth coolness of a morning kiss
Like feathers or a last calm dream.
Or the burn when you stretch your arms,
Arch your shoulders or open out your leg.
The fact of touch, rough and smooth,
Hot and cold, connections as of iron.

Iron at the heart of steel,
The iron in your blood, red and heavy,
An iron age, this time of heavy blows,
Pig iron and iron polished and rigid,
Iron that cuts, the iron that binds.

A gift of iron:
Love wound like the hard strands of a cable,
Taut with weight, or the hair fine coil of a wire,
The string of a guitar or picture wire,
Or the new shapes of fused iron,
Gleaming on the lawn or cool in shadows.
Hand on hand in hand, we hold, fast as iron,

Steady as iron, flowing like fresh water,
Still as a pond, moving like molten iron.

Things to Look At

for Maeryn

1.
A shell you found on the beach,
Half covered in sand. It was late evening,
And the sun wavered red and lonely in the slow sea.
You were alone, and the air was as quiet as water.

And, of course, you lost it,
Left it in the corner of the room
Or behind the white pitcher.
Or perhaps you dropped it,
A curl of calcium in the white sand,
Pink and sharp and circling,
As clean as water or white sand.

A shell you found on the beach
And knew it to see. You see
It now and know the edges of the eye,
A line of damp sand, the returning sea.

2.
A lithograph:
It is hanging by a tall window with heavy drapes.
The light in the room is weak,
And you must lean close to the pale colors.
And then you see it all:
A juggler, an outline of pink,
His teeth are like marbles,
His eyes are moving like balls,
And the balls hang in the air before him
Like an egg of air, you see them hum.
Two children, sisters or friends,
Perhaps they are strangers,
But they squeeze each other,
Their hair like stacked hay,
Their eyes open like windows on blue sky,

47

Watch an oval of air, the juggler's surprise.
And there is a blue sky with dissolving clouds,
And light green grass underfoot,
And in the distance you see a cow,
Head bowed to the grass, or maybe a horse,
It is brown and indistinct.
The juggler's feet are like brown earth,
Solid and set, bare, his toes planted like bulbs,
But he turns the air in his hands.
You are so close your breath clouds the scene
To pink and blue and yellow and green,
But it will clear and does,
A pink juggler set on green ground
Spinning a blue day for little girls,
Their hair as yellow as hay,
In a dim room in an old house
As you walk lightly away.

3.
This spring, last week,
The day so bright and green
After a week of rain
That your eyes are dazzled,
Are dazed.

The grass is raw green
And tassling by the road,
Broken by dark tufts,
The bossed circles
Where fairies dance,
Moon drunk and dizzy
From moonlight into day.
You are driving slowly,
For you know the way.

The trees enclose the road,
They arch and you think
Of green glass, of light
Through green glass
Swimming in stone aisles,
Of high stone arches
And columns cool to the touch.

And ahead is a circle of white:

White pigeons, rock doves
As white as Spanish doves,
Eyes like the tips of matches,
A burst of white feathers
Rising before you.
And they fly the road,
Afloat in green light,
A white escort, a bray
Of trumpets, white banners,
They lead you through leaves
To the hot clap of day.

4.

The way the eager dog,
After he has jumped up to greet you
And wagged his tail out
And bumped his head under your hand
(A pat or quick scratch will do)
More than once, will settle
Like a warm breeze or evening flower,
Perhaps on the red rug by the window
Or against your foot, will stretch out
At length or lower his head (looking up),
Or will lie poised and alert,
His front paws crossed, an X,
And will look you steady eye to eye.

5.

A thunder storm, tonight, lightning
As regular as an electrical sign,
A roar and rattle like an avalanche,
The windows slapped with unsteady rain,
Even the floor rocked and shaken.
The kind of storm Victor Frankenstein
Watched "with curiosity and delight,"
The snapping of night with broken days,
Light gone wild sealing earth and sky,
Cloud to cloud, tree to air, air to ground.

You are safe in the center of the room,
But you press your hand against the glass.
It trembles like a cold wet dog
Or the salty steel plates of a ship.
You see yourself in the glass in the night,

Disappearing in a sudden flash, trees, grass,
And then your face again, warm and dry,
The room behind you, bright lamps,
Your eyes lit, curious with delight.

6.

A train station, a large one,
You know that it is raining outside,
The crowd is large, too, and uneasy,
They move past you in clumsy circles,
And you are alone except for luggage,
Suitcases, leather suitcases, cloth ones,
Uncrushable blue and red suitcases,
And dressbags of shiny plastic,
The hangers snaring the clothes
Of passers-by, hatboxes stacked and uneven,
Brief cases stuffed with valuable papers,
Diagrams, maps, manuscripts,
All of them unique, irreplaceable,
And you are alone with your luggage,
(This is a dream, you are sure of it),
The voice on the loudspeaker is a jumble
And everyone is watching you cry.

You are alone with your luggage,
The mound is as tall as your head,
Taller, and you hear the voice break
Into sudden sense, it names your train,
You take handles and hooks, you push
Cases and boxes with your feet,
You try, you try, you are alone
With your luggage but you try.

And then, doffing caps like a parade
(You are the grandstand) they arrive,
Porters, porters in red caps,
Porters in blue caps and green caps,
Porters in brass buttons, one porter
Tapdances three suitcases away,
Porters with dressbags, and porters
With armloads of hats, porters
Humming, three are whistling together,
Thirty porters whisk your luggage away,
And two in pink caps take your elbows,

They load you aboard like a handbag,
Hundreds of porters who wave you to your seat,
Hundreds of dancing porters. You are amazed.

You are sure that it must be a dream.

7.
You are by yourself,
Sitting in the grass under a tree,
The shade like a circle around you.
The afternoon is warm and very slow.
You have been thinking how dreams change
When they come to be, how they disappoint
Or simply fade away.

And you see a bright butterfly,
Golden and royal red, like sunlight,
Like the bright center of sunlight,
Touching the white blossoms of clover
And hovering like a stillness of air.

Your dream:
That he will land on your finger,
That if you are still as a blossom
He will settle on your finger,
Will tremble there like light on water,
Like sunlight on rippling water.

But the butterfly fades like a dream,
Like the afternoon, flies out of sight,
Around a bush or into deep shade.
Your mind wanders, you drift
Out of focus.

There is another butterfly,
Dark purple, blue black,
The color of a new bruise,
Dusty and dark, flying from flowers,
Flying to your finger like a drunk,
Weaving, wobbling to his left,
And he lands. You are amazed.

This butterfly will not leave.
He is ugly and strange, he stands
On your finger like a blot.
You brush him away, but he clings

Like a shadow or a stain.
His wings waver like the arms
Of a man balancing on a fence,
But he balances, he stays.
Your dream has entered the day
Like a dark surprise.

The sun is golden and yellow.
Clovers dot the wide green grass.
There is a butterfly on your finger,
Like the cool center of shade,
But he is as warm as sunlight, as steady
As a tidal sea. He remains.
He is like the day that holds you,
The air that wraps you round.
The afternoon lengthens and deepens.
You are sitting in the tree's green shadow.
There is a butterfly on your finger.

You are everything that you could ever wish to be.

Emerson, Poe and Borges

Incredibly, within twenty seconds, they had left
fire, smoke, their fate and their death behind.
            —Ellery Queen

I.
(*After the Spanish of Jorge Luis Borges*)

The sun draws out the afternoon
As long as its shadow.
You are thinking of Emerson,
How that tall American must have found a day as long,
How he must have closed his book,
His marked copy of Montaigne,
How he must have walked out into the sunlight,
Toward the sunlight, the last sharp edge of the day.
You shape his thoughts
As he walks the wide pampas of your mind:

I have read the books that I must
And written others that will outlast this day.
I have been given all that a man may know.
My name circles the globe,
But I have not lived.
I would be another man.

Then Emerson fades in the dusk.
A bat skips the air by your face
Like a stone.
You turn to go inside.
You think: I have not lived.
I would be another man.

Your face examines you
From the clear glass of your door.

II.
(After the Spanish of Jorge Luis Borges)

That night you think of Poe
Who did not fear the night.
You see him carved in black marble,
The ivy inching its way up the stone
Like worms that measure the grave.
Poe never feared earth or the worm:
He only feared the luck of the day,
The luck that gives you love
And takes that love away—
Not the dark stone, but a single yellow rose.

Poe's is the face on the other side of the glass,
There with the nightmares he shaped by hand,
With things and thoughts,
With silence and shadow, the turning rim of the pool.

You think of him on the other side of death:
Alone, silent, strong, making marvels
Both splendid and atrocious.

The wind opens the curtains at your window.
The night is moonless.
You hear the quiet movement of water.

III.

The next morning you are Borges:
Borges waking, Borges at breakfast,
Borges walking toward the sunlight,
Borges afoot in the rising dew.

You, too, have made marvels,
Written words that will last,
And you have recognized the face
In the mandala of your lines.

You are in a world of forms,
Shapes of the open day,
They glow like new coins.

You walk as precisely as the edge of a knife,
You are light as air.

You are thinking of two gauchos,
How words echo like the jingle of spurs,
Of what you must say, how you have seen
All that a man may know, how when you reach the curb
You will stop and listen carefully,
And cross the avenue, walk in the formal trees
Until you reach the wide river,
The clear water silent as moving glass.

Scratching the Stuffed Dog's Ear

Closed as a closet door,
Locked and the key lost for years,
No word, not a sound,
Only the sensation of air.

An exploration:
The only map a single line
As far as a man may reach,
The trickle of fingers
Down a slick wall,
A measure of bootlengths,
An echo that trembles in the ear.

Memories:
The blue of sky behind a green cedar,
The crumbs of mortar between red bricks,
The stubble of yellow hairs high on her leg,
The dark click of teeth in a kiss,
The blue cedar at dusk.

Likenesses:
A snake in the road like raw muscle,
A knife with the curve of a snake,
A road that blurs like water,
Cold water that dulls like a knife,
The muscle that tugs at an eye.

A discovery:
Another way in, a way out,
Change in a pocket, the key,
A map in every palm,
The secret of chimneys,
A hollow panel, a passage,
Another way out.

The sensation of air:
An exchange,
A communion,
The banging open of a door,
A bound of light,
A rush of weather,
An explosion into sound.

Gettysburg

for Bruce and Betsy Stefany

It don't hurt a bit to be shot in a wooden leg.
—Lt. Gen. Richard S. Ewell, CSA

It is a swelling and falling away of ground,
Stones and stone, the trees lined up along the wall,
And an accumulation of names.

Gettysburg has an echo
Like a shout in rocks.

You hear it
Even when you look away.

Say Spangler's Spring or Culp's Hill,
The Round Tops, the Angle,
Say the Devil's Den,
Say Cemetery Hill.

Fifty thousand hit in July,
Down in Pennsylvania farm dirt.
Richard Dillard felt his leg collapse
With a bright stain like a fallen flag.
Home is just over the hill, they said,
And two years later it was.

We'll fight them, sir, till hell freezes over,
And then, sir, we'll fight them on the ice.

Too bad, Lee said, too bad.
Oh, too bad. And then the rain
Slid down the butts of rifles,
Down the barrels and bayonet blades
And into the ground, the first drops
Dancing in the dust like live things,
Then a rush that laid all dust to rest.

The real war was somewhere to the west.
This one was only a dream, a spring
Of dreams, dreams that still splash
Like living things on the ground.

It is ground and grass,
A piling up of names like stones,
It is earth and air, a place to live.
You can move through echoes without a glance
Or drop them like postcards into the box
To be sent on with best wishes.

Or you can walk out Wainwright Avenue,
Past Hancock on his horse, and Slocum,
Slowly, thinking of another day, other days,
Watch the high clouds circle like birds
And hold hands or not this day, as you will.

You feel the muscles in your legs
Climbing Culp's Hill, climbing the tower
On Culp's Hill, feel the blood moving

In them like slow ice or warm as plowed ground.
Names fade in this accumulation of air.
You can see the day turn through the clouds.

If you need to remember anything,
It is the best way home.

Limits

(After the Spanish of Jorge Luis Borges)

The rain holds you in like skin
Or a wall, steady, almost solid.
The brick walls through the trees
Move like dreams or memories.
Your eyes search for sharp things,
Objects with edges, lights like knives.
The day has lost all definition,
Is as closed as some dark lithograph.

You remember:
The rain of May, the rain of July,
The rain of ten years ago in the winter,
A whisper shared in the rain,
How the rain smashes on your shoes
Or its loose rattle on an umbrella,
Rain in weeds or across water,
The taste of rain, the smell,
How her skin is as slick and shiny
In the rain as an apple or plums.

You know:
There is a poem by Borges
You will never remember,
And a street (it curves down the hill)
That is forever closed to you,
At least one door (the knob once warm
With your hand) which you have closed
Until the end of the world.

I know a face which I seek in every stranger's,
Which I shall never see again.
I know there are books in my shelves

(They are all around me now)
Which I shall never open again.
This wet autumn closes my thirty-fourth year.
Death continues to blur and reduce me,
To reduce you as you read this page,
Steadily and as sure as rain.

Surprises

> We cannot stay among the ruins.
> —R. W. Emerson

The sudden edge of a bell
Or a knock. You answer,
If at all, touching wood.

You touch wood, and you answer.
It is like turning a page.
It is the mailman or a boy.
It is the undertaker.
It is Cyndy whom you haven't seen for months
Or Cronan who was just by yesterday.
It is a pirate with someone on his shoulder,
Someone you know.
Or it is Annie who has overlooked her key.

The day dazzles, dances,
The light splashing in like rain.
There are twelve policemen at your door.
There are two men with a cow
Or one man with an eye like a radish.

There is no one at the door at all.

No point in going back to bed.
The day is torn open like an envelope.
It is as open as the door.
You are opening like a door,
Steadying like a zeppelin in the air.
You take on edges. You expand.

Something has come to call
And found you in. And now
You must go calling on the day.

58

After Borges

No force of imagination can convert
us into another person, and make us
fancy, that we, being that person, reap
benefit from those valuable qualities,
which belong to him. Or if it did, no
celerity of imagination could
immediately transport us back, into
ourselves, and make us love and esteem
the person, as different from us.
   —David Hume

These things we share:
Sun, water, earth,
The primary need of air,
The round rhythm of day on day.

These things we gain:
A dream of fire, of a tiger's eye,
The salt desert's glare,
A wisdom of the silent south,
The last labyrinth's one straight line,
Windows, doors, the winding paths
That lead to an open way.

These things we need:
Secrets of Welsh stone in Wiltshire,
Of winds at Egyptian sunset,
Of the reach of grasses at dawn
And sources of shadow at noon,
The strength to walk on water,
The gift of breathing in,
Faith of breathing out,
Fact of the waiting world.

These things we are:
All things, one thing distinct
And nothing more, Borges and I
As different as day from day,
A meeting, a turning away,
Surprise and its sudden result,
A river that flows on to stay.

Round Ruby Too

Round as gloves,
Round Ruby at the door
Causes light to whirl in
Like dancers, polish on the floor
And sawdust, spinning a gavotte
Or a mazurka,
Aware of destinations,
Clanging like a round brass bell,
Bright as Round Ruby,
Round as a glove,
The glove she is pulling on,
She says goodbye,
As sure as yesterday,
Today,
Round Ruby.